wise traveller

loss

meditations for life's journey

© Scripture Union 2007

First published 2007

ISBN 978 1 84427 311 9

207–209 Queensway, Bletchley, Milton Keynes, MK2 2EB, UK
www.wisetraveller.org.uk

British Library Cataloguing-in-Publication Data: a catalogue
record of this book is available from the British Library.

Cover image and text illustrations by Andrew Gray © 2007

The Wise Traveller logo (created by Andrew Gray)
© Scripture Union 2007

Andrew Gray has asserted his right under the Copyright,
Designs and Patents Act 1988, to be identified as the
illustrator of this work.

Cover and internal design and layout by x1.ltd.uk

Printed and bound by Henry Ling Ltd, Dorchester, England

Contents

Introduction

Many of us want a more spiritually satisfying life. This book is about catching hold of those moments of divine intensity that come our way in the midst of everyday living. As David Adam, a writer who draws on the inspiration of the ancient Celts, puts it, 'We need to walk with awe and wonder, we need to be aware of the deep mystery and power that flows through all things. ... We need to discover again that there is an adventure to be lived in our world, a personal discovery to be made of the presence and the life that dances in all things.' And so this book is also about celebrating life as a journey, one which we 'walk with awe and wonder', recognising that there is something about the travelling, as well as the arriving, that should be treasured.

It's not always a popular theme, but by way of contrast to the hedonism of modern life is the view that worthwhile things take time, that process is important, and that taking the long way round cultivates traditional benefits such as patience and perseverance. This is what the journey can do for us. As we walk in solitude or in company we discover the power of the journey to prepare us, resource us and change us in ways that enhance our appreciation of the significant 'arrival' moments in our lives. Sure, it might be easier to drive straight to the packaged tourist experience, but the journey via the coastal path will have many compensations: the changing light on the ocean; the colour and contours of the cliffs; the seabird colonies perched precariously; the white sand draped like a scarf around the bay.

The *Wise Traveller* series offers wisdom for the journey; wisdom drawn from the spiritual classics of the Christian tradition alongside original reflections – stories, poems and meditations – that engage with the spiritual, emotional and, sometimes, brutal realities of life. As Proverbs 24:3,4 (TNIV) says: 'By wisdom a house is built, and through understanding it is established; through knowledge its rooms are filled with rare and beautiful treasures.'

This book has been written and compiled by people who would identify themselves as Christian in the broadest understanding of that term. These are people who have wrestled with what it means to live fully and who, time and time again, have turned to the Bible to find the wisdom, inspiration and guidance they need to carry on. At the back of the book you'll find notes that offer suggestions for further reading, showing where ideas and themes explored in the book originate in these ancient biblical writings that the Christian tradition has always recognised as sacred and God-inspired.

For many of us, seeking deeper fulfilment in life means increasing our sense of peace. This book offers opportunities to nurture stillness through contemplation. As you read, you may find it helpful to pause and reflect on your thoughts and feelings using the 'litany' or devotional pattern provided, a line of which appears on the first page of each chapter, accompanied by a woodblock-style illustration for those of us who find art a stimulus to meditation. The litany is inspired by the famous Celtic prayer, 'St Patrick's Breastplate', whose author, understanding Jesus to be the Son of God, calls upon him to be his companion and friend on each step of the journey:

Christ be with me, Christ within me,
Christ behind me, Christ before me,
Christ beside me, Christ to win me,
Christ to comfort and restore me.
Christ beneath me, Christ above me,

Christ in quiet, Christ in danger,
Christ in hearts of all that love me,
Christ in mouth of friend and stranger.

Whatever your spiritual convictions and hopes, I hope this collection blesses you on life's journey.

Phil Andrews
Series Editor

Other titles available in the *Wise Traveller* series:

Happiness

Relationships

Yet to be published:

Forgiveness

Growing

Hope

Griever

I see the path ahead of me...

Affliction makes God appear to be absent for a time, more absent than a dead man, more absent than light in the utter darkness of a cell. A kind of horror submerges the whole soul.

During this absence there is nothing to love.

What is terrible is that if, in this darkness where there is nothing to love, the soul ceases to love, God's absence becomes final.

The soul has to go on loving in the emptiness, or at least to go on wanting to love, though it may only be with an infinitesimal part of itself. Then, one day, God will come to show himself to this soul and to reveal the beauty of the world to it, as in the case of Job.

But if the soul stops loving it falls, even in this life, into something which is almost equivalent to hell.

Simone Weil (1909-1943)

Though I walk more and more slowly

Though some days I can't be bothered to walk at all

Though I sleepwalk as if it's all a bad dream

Though I walk and trip and fall and wonder if I will

Ever get up again

Though I walk as if these are the last steps I will ever take

Because I will never walk with you again

Though I walk with a limp

Dragging along this leaden heart, this heavy life

Though I walk on an earth where I will never hold you or

be held by you

Never call you or be called by you

Though I walk through a valley from which all light has

been evacuated

Where familiar paths have disappeared, lost from view

Still

God is with me

Though I walk through the valley of the shadow

Where despair encircles like hounds

Where darkness seems my only companion

Still

God is with me, I will fear no evil

Though I walk through the valley of the shadow

Surely goodness and mercy

Shall follow me

Surely they can't be far behind

Surely they will catch me up

Surely they will bring me home

Martin Wroe

Revealer

I see the road behind me...

I am with you always.

When the crushing pain of doubt sets in

and you feel utterly, utterly alone,

I am with you.

When you are screaming why at the sky

and the pain sears through you

like a soldier's spear,

I am with you.

When everything you had

trickles like sand through your fingers,

I am with you.

When your plans are in shreds,

I am with you.

Always

I am here.

Sue Wallace

I pray and incur
silence. Some take that silence
for refusal.

I feel the power
that, invisible, catches me
by the sleeve, nudging
towards the long shelf
that has the book on it I will take down
and read and find the antidote
to an ailment.

I know its ways with me;
how it enters my life,
is present rather
before I perceive it, sunlight quivering
on a bare wall.

Is it consciousness trying
to get through?

        Am I under
regard?
        It takes me seconds
to focus, by which time
        it has shifted its gaze,
looking to one
        side, as though I were not here.

It has the universe
        to be abroad in.
There is nothing I can do
but fill myself with my own
        silence, hoping it will approach
        like a wild creature to drink
there or, perhaps like Narcissus
to linger a moment over its transparent face.

RS Thomas (1913-2000)

Opportunity-taker

I see the land around me...

remember the autumn when, as a child, I discovered conkers. It was amazing! Nestling beneath a horse chestnut tree was a host of spiky packages. I peeled each of them open to reveal a ready-carved and newly-polished wooden egg, rich and shiny, with red veins streaking its veneer.

On that first day I rushed around collecting armfuls of them, to set down on my bedside table like precious jewels; resolving that I was never going to give them away. Then each morning afterwards I'd wake up and admire them. They were so beautiful! Yet as time passed, a horrible change came over them. After a while they began to shrink and warp. The red veins disappeared and they shrivelled into hard, brown, lumpy little stones. Deeply disappointed, I threw my 'jewels' away.

With hindsight I don't know why I didn't try planting them instead of trying to preserve them as they were. Then, with a little nurturing, perhaps I could have seen the birth of a new tree, a treasure box of potential.

Sue Wallace

The last time I saw you, I wish we'd talked about the day of the picnic. It had been a glorious day and we'd spent all morning preparing the food. It made quite a spread when it was laid out. Then, as if it had been deliberately waiting for maximum effect, the heavens opened. Our food and our clothes were soaked in seconds. You just began laughing and soon I started laughing too, both of us sitting there in the rain with our sodden banquet laughing and laughing.

It was so good to see you laugh; you rarely found much to laugh about. Often, instead, you would tell me once more how ashamed you were of me, or how I should've worked at school. I would then respond as always by blaming you for ruining my life; telling you how it had felt to grow up with parents who were always fighting, and how impossible you were when you got drunk. And so we would argue. There was no laughter the last time I saw you.

The last time I saw you I wish I'd told you I loved you, and holding you close that I'd forgiven you. I knew how hurt inside you were too. I wish that had happened instead of the shouting, the stamped feet and the slamming door. But I didn't know it was the last time I'd see you, we didn't know how ill you were. *Did you?* If only I'd known the last time I saw you. So I'm saying now the things I wish I'd told you. I don't know if where you have gone you can hear me, but I hope it's a place in which you are laughing again. If you can hear me, hear what I really feel, forgive me for what I said the last time I saw you. And if there is a place where we will meet again and be able to say all the things face to face we didn't say before, then the next time I see you will be so much better than the last time I saw you.

Steve Hollinghurst

Consoler

I see who travels with me...

What now remains? To bring the healing of the Word to those in sorrow. And a powerful remedy for mourners is sympathy, for sufferers are best consoled by those who have to bear a like suffering. To such, then, I specially address myself, of whom I should be ashamed, if, with all other virtues, they do not show the elements of patience. For even if they surpass all others in love of their children, let them equally surpass them in love of wisdom and love of Christ, and in the special practice of meditation on our departure hence, impressing it likewise on their children, making even their whole life a preparation for death. ... How much longer have we to live, ye men of honoured eld, so near to God? How long are we to suffer here? Not even man's whole life is long, compared with the Eternity of the Divine Nature, still less the remains of life, and what I may call the parting of our human breath, the close of our frail existence.

St Gregory of Nazianzus (329–389)

'O death, where is thy sting?' shouts one Christian scripture, with far more confidence than I usually have when staring loss in the face. And I am a Church of England priest...

Even those who have great faith in eternal life feel the pain of loss. It's hard not to when you spend a lot of time with grieving people. If we want to talk about death unsentimentally, then we have to accept that death actually stings very sharply.

Death stings through the feeling of devastation we have when someone close to us passes away. Death stings through anger too, if the loss seemed untimely or unjust. Death stings through anxieties about what a suddenly emptied future holds.

As a clergyman I often drop in on the relatives of one recently deceased. They will say, 'We've got Dad in the front room if you'd like to go and see him.' It's not an offer you can refuse, even if every sinew of your spirit is pulling you the opposite way. Being a religious professional doesn't make it any easier.

And so, in your complete incomprehension and overwhelming sense of inadequacy in the face of absolute mortality, you stand beside a white cloth decorated with roses and look down on the dearly loved and lost one and find yourself talking inanely whilst an alternative – critical – commentary plays out in your head.

'Doesn't he look peaceful?' you say (whilst thinking to yourself, *of course he looks peaceful, you fool, he's dead!*).

'He would have liked having his family here with him tonight' you say (whilst thinking, *he'd have liked it a lot more if he'd still been here with his family tonight!*).

My experience is the same as for any visitor to a bereaved family. Somehow your visit consoles the mourners. Perhaps because they appreciate that you've opted, however reluctantly, to share your uselessness and vulnerability with them. They understand that all you can do is stand together in the face of death, feeling the rawness of the moment.

Death does have a sting, and our journey sometimes brings us to pause alongside those who have been newly stung by it.

John Davies

Fellow traveller

I see the ground beneath me...

In this darkness
I do not ask to walk by light;
but to feel the touch of your hand
and understand that sight is not seeing.

In this silence
I do not ask to hear your voice;
but to sense your Spirit breathe
and know myself a word of your speaking.

In unknowing
I do not ask for fearless space;
but for grace to comprehend
that neither you or I are diminished.

In this death
I do not seek escape from pain;
but embracing loss, to find
the strength to cross the bridge of waiting.

Pat Bennett

The Christian Gospels include a story about two men travelling from Jerusalem, full of grief and shock, following the horrific death of their spiritual leader, Jesus. A stranger draws alongside them and asks them what the matter is, and listens to their story as they pour out their bewilderment and loss. We are too often frightened by the grief and pain of others and do not draw close to them. We say it's 'being sensitive' but actually the opposite is true.

The stranger on the Emmaus road then shared a message that comforted the grieving men and was based on the beliefs they all shared. It told how Jesus' violent death was not without purpose and that there was reason to go on hoping. The travellers never wrote down the message they received; perhaps because what mattered was the hope they received in their despair. They were beyond noting down specific details, anyway.

It seems only natural to try to find meaning in such losses, but so hard when it seems 'pointless' like Jesus' death – a holy man murdered by the corrupt and jealous. Perhaps, then, what we need in our grief is not words that seek to explain away our pain but ones that give us hope in the midst of it. As the two men reached the place they were to stay on their journey they invited the stranger to join them, such being the support he had been to them in their grief. He appears to have changed his plans to eat with them, though perhaps he anticipated the invitation. I wonder if the grieving men feared the other would be all too pleased to move on from their mournful company. It is perhaps in the times of not saying anything, of being together doing normal things like sharing a meal, that company is most needed and hardest to give. And it was then, as he broke the bread, that they recognised him and he vanished from their sight.

The resurrected Jesus no doubt had many things to do, a miracle to proclaim, but he chose to walk gently alongside these two ordinary men in their grief. Ever since, for any who care to notice, he still walks alongside those who suffer.

Steve Hollinghurst

Truth-teller

I see the sky above me...

called to mind the Prophet who shouted, 'I am but earth and ash.' And once again I looked with attention on the tombs, and I saw the bones therein which of flesh were naked; and I said, 'Which indeed is he that is king? Or which is soldier? Which is the wealthy, which the needy? Which the righteous, or which the sinner?' But to Your servant, O Lord, grant that with the righteous he may repose.

St John of Damascus (c676–749)

The great king Solomon, legend has it, was the wisest of all kings. In his youth he wrote love poetry so beautiful that it entered the canon of Jewish sacred writings. In middle age he wrote proverbs to guide the traveller, and in later years, a lament full of aged wisdom.

A story is told around the campfires about Solomon. One day, it goes, Solomon issued his jeweller with a challenge.

'I want a ring,' he said, 'that will speak truth on every occasion. When I give it to a laughing traveller, their mood will become solemn, yet when I give it to a suffering soul, they will smile once more.'

The jeweller thought and worked long and hard for many months. The task seemed impossible. Finally, on the brink of giving up, he had a flash of inspiration, and set to work...

He took the finished ring to the king who smiled as he reached out to take hold of the golden band. Yet as he peered down to read the inscription that ran around it Solomon's face fell and tears filled his eyes, for the words he read were, 'This too shall pass'.

Surrounded by all his riches and glory, King Solomon had been struck by the realisation that it would one day all end, that his life was fragile, that every moment was precious.

In his sadness the king gazed at the inscription once more. 'This too will pass,' he repeated aloud. Then he realised… this meant that he would not feel sad for ever! His tears would dry, and he would smile again.

'Well done, jeweller,' Solomon said. 'This ring surely speaks the truth.'

Just then Solomon's wife, who had been listening in an anteroom, entered, and seeing the golden circle shining in the sunlight, exclaimed, 'This ring does indeed speak the truth, husband, for it speaks of unending love, a circle with no beginning and no end. Love that can never pass, though the earth itself crumbles.'

Solomon kissed his wife and said, 'You too have spoken truly. For all things must pass, and yet love is eternal.'

Sue Wallace

Sacrificer

I see the path ahead of me...

The ultimate measure of a man is not where he stands in moments of comfort and convenience, but where he stands at times of challenge and controversy. The true neighbour will risk his position, his prestige, and even his life for the welfare of others. In dangerous valleys and hazardous pathways, he will lift some bruised and beaten neighbour to a higher and more noble life.

Martin Luther King, Jr (1929-1968)

If it's stolen from you
If it's broken by you
If it's special to you
If it cost a lot;
If it's all you had
If it was just a whim
If it's gone and won't come back:
I will take responsibility for your loss.

When you couldn't care less about it
When you couldn't care more
When your world depends on it
When it finds you uninsured;
When it was a gift you rejected
When it was a joy undiscovered
When it was an inevitable collapse:
I will take responsibility for your loss.

Even if it will hurt me

Even if it will humble me

Even if it will choke me

Even if it will exploit me;

Even if it will anger me

Even if it will disgrace me

Even if it will kill me:

I will take responsibility for your loss.

John Davies

Transformer

I see the road behind me...

I once heard a story in which a woman was given a quest, to find a house death had not visited. She failed in her task. It was an impossible one. And this started me thinking. If I was given the task of finding a person who had never suffered loss, would I be able to do it? I thought about it and decided I would find a newborn baby. Surely they could never have suffered loss? Then, later, when I came to look into the eyes of a bawling child I imagined them speaking a very different answer to the one I'd assumed: 'I was surrounded by warmth and love and comfort. I had everything I ever wanted, and then in a flash my world changed! I was forced into a strange, cold, scary place of noise and light and fear. I had been born but it felt like dying, for I'd lost my whole world.'

Sue Wallace

We do not have to deny or avoid our loneliness, our hostilities and illusions. To the contrary: When we have the courage to let these realities come to our full attention, understand them and confess them, then they can slowly be converted into solitude, hospitality and prayer.

This does not imply that a mature spiritual life is a life in which our old lonely hostile self with all its illusions disappears and we live in complete serenity with a peaceful mind and a pure heart. Just as our adulthood shows the marks or the struggles of our youth, so our solitude bears the signs of the lonely hours, our care for others reflects at times angry feelings and our prayer sometimes reveals the memory and the presence of many illusions.

Transformed in love, however, these painful signs become signs of hope, as the wounds of Jesus did for the doubting Thomas.

Henri Nouwen (1932-1996)

It's a long way off but inside it
There are quite different things going on·
Festivals at which the poor man
Is king and the consumptive is
Healed; mirrors in which the blind look
At themselves and love looks at them
Back; and industry is for mending
The bent bones and the minds fractured
By life. It's a long way off, but to get
There takes no time and admission
Is free, if you will purge yourself
Of desire, and present yourself with
Your need only and the simple offering
Of your faith, green as a leaf.

RS Thomas (1913–2000)

Restorer

I see the land around me...

If you do away with the yoke of oppression,

with the pointing finger and malicious talk,

and if you spend yourselves on behalf of the hungry

and satisfy the needs of the oppressed,

then your light will rise in the darkness,

and your night will become like the noonday.

The LORD will guide you always;

he will satisfy your needs in a sun-scorched land

and will strengthen your frame.

You will be like a well-watered garden,

like a spring whose waters never fail.

Your people will rebuild the ancient ruins

and will raise up the age-old foundations;

you will be called Repairer of Broken Walls,

Restorer of Streets with Dwellings.

Isaiah 58:9b–12
(The Bible, Today's New International Version)

A loss can be the cause of conflict. Not long ago a young man from inner Liverpool stole a Mercedes from an outlying suburb, span it out of control at a roundabout and died in an instant pyre while his girlfriend, with horrible spinal injuries, crawled from the burning wreckage. His body was barely recognisable and one of the region's busiest sections of road was closed for 24 hours for forensic investigations.

Over the coming days the death scene became a shrine to the deceased, as family and friends performed the contemporary custom of placing flowers, photographs and personal items by the scorched trees that had taken the impact of the crash.

Meanwhile, the people of the well-heeled suburb became restless. Voices were raised about the shrine's inappropriateness. Police agreed that it may be a distraction to passing drivers, a road safety issue. Community leaders listened sympathetically to those saying that roadside tributes were morbid, but tiptoed carefully around the issues raised by sharper voices protesting that the shrine should not be there because the deceased was a thief.

These voices were influential. Their harsh insistence gave the impression that they represented the majority. Rumours flew around the town that the burgled family's 5-year-old daughter was traumatised, that the police operation at the crash cost a million pounds. The dead man's aunt told the press that he wasn't malicious, just too easily led – a nice, easy-going lad, not a career criminal.

Days before the funeral, friends of the dead man picnicked on the roundabout, to the outrage of some local residents. On the day of the funeral the shrine was trashed and a memorial plaque from the scene was posted to the local newspaper office with the words 'scum' and 'thief' scratched into it. Days after, a new shrine appeared at the scene.

The fatal roundabout has become a place where these things are painfully contested: crime and punishment, inequality and social dislocation, tribalism and local identities, justice and grace. What you think was lost where that crash happened depends a lot on how you arrived there.

John Davies

Voyager

I see who travels with me...

Why no! I never thought other than
That God is that great absence
In our lives, the empty silence
Within, the place where we go
Seeking, not in hope to
Arrive or find. He keeps the interslices
In our knowledge, the darkness
Between stars. His are the echoes
We follow, the footprints he has just
Left. We put our hands in
His side hoping to find
It warm. We look at people
And places as though he had looked
At them, too; but miss the reflection.

RS Thomas (1913–2000)

In 1972, the year of my birth, the last booster ignited and propelled the last landing module up from the surface of the moon to glide silently through the thin-air darkness and meet the last command module. For the last time that tube of tin-can electronics pointed its nose back at the thumbnail earth in the far distance, shot through space and back into the comforting arms of earth's orbit.

We are 6 billion or so here, with common rock under all our feet. Only 21 have ever properly left home, actually escaped fully the drag of our world's gravity; only 12 from 6 billion have placed their feet on the surface of a truly foreign land.

Their wonder, their transport, was a rocket comprising 3 million components all with a 99.9 per cent success rate. Which meant that, in any given launch, around 3,000 parts were likely to fail. Somehow, none ever did. For some reason, these men sat over 100 metres up, atop 3,000 tonnes of propellant, ready to be fired like peas from a cannon.

Why?

In his book *Moondust*, the author Andrew Smith went in search of those who remained to ask them. Navy pilots, aeronautics experts, astronomy graduates, scientists. These rational minds who coolly followed launch patterns and calmly told Houston if they had a problem were now lost for words. 'Lunatics' all, going mad back on earth wondering why NASA wouldn't let them return to where eyes saw 20 times more clearly and little leaps could be metres.

Will we ever go back? Why did we stop?

These moon-landers are the naïve believers in us all, walkers on rare places, temporary inhabitants of a smaller, simpler world.

Their grief is our common latent loss, the human ache for the part of us that once flew divinely. Now we stand with leaden feet, wings clipped, staring at the stars, wondering. We must breathe this heavier air for a while, and experience the weight of a whole life lived before we are allowed to return. We will be wiser then.

Kester Brewin

Uprooter

I see the ground beneath me...

By faith Abraham obeyed when he was called to go out to a place that he was to receive as an inheritance. And he went out, not knowing where he was going. By faith he went to live in the land of promise, as in a foreign land, living in tents with Isaac and Jacob, heirs with him of the same promise. For he was looking forward to the city that has foundations, whose designer and builder is God. By faith Sarah herself received power to conceive, even when she was past the age, since she considered him faithful who had promised. Therefore from one man, and him as good as dead, were born descendants as many as the stars of heaven and as many as the innumerable grains of sand by the seashore.

These all died in faith, not having received the things promised, but having seen them and greeted them from afar, and having acknowledged that they were strangers and exiles on the earth. For people who speak thus make it clear that they are seeking a homeland.

Hebrews 11:8-14 (The Bible, English Standard Version)

You think you know somewhere. You might, for instance, think you 'know' North Wales – a postcard place; a happy place. And then you stand by the A487, the coast road between Aberystwyth and Cardigan, and you see the words 'Cofiwch Dryweryn' ('Remember Tryweryn') daubed in white letters on what remains of a cowshed.

For 40 years or so now, that paint has kept on being renewed, the words reappearing again and again on the mouldering reddish stonework; the ivy being clipped back. Whoever is doing this really, really wants you to remember. Remember that in the late 1950s there was a place near Bala called the Tryweryn Valley, and that by the end of the next decade it had become the floor of a reservoir to feed the cities of England. People marched. People protested. The anger flowed like the waters:

'This ... is one of the most creative communities in the whole of Wales ... Do not wonder then at the anger of the Welsh when Liverpool calmly proclaims its purpose of putting an immense waterworks in the heart of the valley.'

'... It was the drowning of a valley, in what we've come to call the heartlands of Wales. The chapel, the streets, would disappear beneath the waters, and it was a terrible thought to a lot of people.'

It is the past now – you cannot go there. The villagers left. The farms are gone (some would still say 'stolen'). In their place just memories and mournful anger. And a white paint lament for an Eden that was lost.

Matt Campbell

Home-comer

I see the sky above me...

If you find me please don't blame me
I have spent too long in pity and anger and regret
I am to blame I know, though not only me
But I am long past passing the blame
So please don't add to my shame
Please forgive me and do it gently if you find me

If you find me please don't turn your back on me
I know I turned my back on you and you might
    do the same
But I want to see you smile with arms
    open welcoming me
I want to come home and be with you again
And if in finding me you will indeed behave this way
Please come looking for me, for I'm lost and
    I need you to find me.

Steve Hollinghurst

Israel was taken into exile in 587 BC. The people were uprooted from the place in which they were born. The land that had been promised to them, which they had possessed, in which their identity as a people of God had been formed, was gone. In the new land, Babylon, customs were strange, the language incomprehensible, and the landscape oddly flat and featureless.

Israel's exile was a violent and extreme form of what all of us experience from time to time. Inner experiences of exile take place even if we never move from the street on which we were brought up. Experiences of exile, minor and major, continue through changes in society, changes in government, changes in values, changes in our bodies, our emotions, our families and marriages.

Daily we face decisions on how we will respond to these exile conditions. We can say: 'I don't like it; I want to be where I was ten years ago. How can you expect me to throw myself into what I don't like – that would be sheer hypocrisy. What sense is there in taking risks and tiring myself out among people I don't even like in a place where I have no future?'

Or we can say: 'I will do my best with what is here Far more important than the climate of this place, the economics of this place, the neighbours in this place, is the God of this place. God is here with me. What I am experiencing right now is on ground that was created by him and with people whom he loves. It is just as possible to live out the will of God here as any place else. I am full of fear. I have much to learn. I'm not sure I can make it. But I had feelings like that back in Jerusalem. Change is hard. Developing intimacy among strangers is always a risk. Building relationships in unfamiliar and hostile surroundings is difficult. But if that is what it means to be alive and human I will do it.'

Eugene H Peterson

Seeker

I see the path ahead of me...

God wants us to worship Him. He doesn't need us, for He couldn't be a self-sufficient God and need anything or anybody, but He wants us. When Adam sinned it was not he who cried, 'God, where art Thou?' It was God who cried, 'Adam, where art thou?'

AW Tozer (1897-1963)

She had the whole restaurant on our knees, looking for it. The earring that had become dislodged somewhere between the doorway and her table, and had evidently bounced away under someone's feet.

We just had to find it, the other customers, because there were tears rolling down this young woman's face, and great distress in her voice at the thought of losing this precious thing.

This did not take place in an expensive eatery, tastefully lit and with a delicate ambience. Those trying to find the distressed woman's lost earring were not the most urbane diners, and this was not a special occasion for her, or for anyone else involved in this micro-drama.

This all happened in a roadside service station, under the blaze of strip lights in the middle of an ordinary day. The customers involved were mostly eating processed food from cardboard containers, and with the exception of one childminder and her 3-year-old charges, they were all just passing through, refuelling.

So it came as little surprise that, when the earring was retrieved by the painter-decorator in the corner seat beneath the TV screen, those who watched him return it to the deeply grateful woman noticed that this earring was very ordinary, nothing special at all.

The young woman, wiping the tears from her cheeks, noticed the people's reactions and offered an explanation.

'I know it's only a cheap thing,' she said unapologetically, 'but it was my best friend's, you see. I was with her when she bought it; it cost her £6.50. But she loved it. It really matched the colour of her eyes. And she died last month. Cancer. But when she was ill she gave this to me. It means a lot...'

No loss is insignificant. And exceptional stories play out beneath the loss of small things, in the most ordinary of places.

John Davies

Simplifier

I see the road behind me...

Has anyone by fussing in front of the mirror ever gotten taller by so much as an inch? All this time and money wasted on fashion – do you think it makes that much difference? Instead of looking at the fashions, walk out into the fields and look at the wildflowers. They never primp or shop, but have you ever seen color and design quite like it? The ten best-dressed men and women in the country look shabby alongside them.

If God gives such attention to the appearance of wildflowers – most of which are never even seen – don't you think he'll attend to you, take pride in you, do his best for you? What I'm trying to do here is to get you to relax, to not be so preoccupied with getting, so you can respond to God's giving. People who don't know God and the way he works fuss over these things, but you know both God and how he works. Steep your life in God-reality, God-initiative, God-provisions. Don't worry about missing out. You'll find all your everyday human concerns will be met.

Matthew 6:27-33 (The Bible, The Message version)

It's only through losing your life that you'll gain it.' Surely this is nonsense, isn't it? Aren't we here to gather around us shoes and jewellery and larger houses and faster cars and collect them behind walled gardens and wrought iron gates just like the celebs do – a window display of all our successes for everyone to see?

A simple calculation dividing the habitable parts of the earth's surface by the population would give each of us a piece of land about the size of a football field. We could all have space for a huge house, with a swimming pool, with probably some green space left over to grow some food. We could gather all our possessions onto this little personal dominion, climb atop the pile with some new flag and declare ourselves President.

There are some problems with this, of course: we'd need roads between the plots to deliver stuff. And probably an airport too. And a place to put the factories. And some way of powering it all. All eating into my space. And people would still need to go and make all this stuff for me, and I'd probably need some way to pay for it.

Before long our island dream dissolves back into our two-up, two-down, with a garden if we're lucky. A play-off between wanting objects and needing people to produce them.

An old man in the desert was said to have had just a begging bowl and, one lucky day, a bag of rice. A robber came by and snatched the old man's rice. The old man got up and raced after him. He caught the robber and lent on his shoulder, panting. 'Here,' he said, 'you forgot to take my begging bowl too.'

He had understood the lie that possessions tell: they boast that they will make us more popular, but they only serve to insulate us further from the human warmth we all really need. This is the gain we make when we strip our lives bare: there is nothing to separate us.

Kester Brewin

Loser

I see the land around me...

I'm having to admit that some of my dreams will never be fulfilled. There are a number of careers I'm already too late for; footballers and stock traders have retired by my age. When I was young and opportunities seemed endless there was no pressure to know where I was going and what I really wanted to do. Now I'm starting to know what to aim for just as my choices are diminishing. As I look ahead I fear I'm destined to reach old age knowing exactly what it was I was supposed to have done while no longer being able to ever do it.

We are defined in our world by what we do and the thought of 'having done nothing with my life' scares me. But should this be so? In the end when I'm not 'doing' anything it'll be who I am that defines me. Will I like who I am? Do I like who I am now? Perhaps as my options reduce the most important opportunity of all lies open: to become a person worth growing old with.

Steve Hollinghurst

It is not easy to lose your life
Without becoming dead
But it is still worth trying
In order to really find yourself

It is not easy to discover that there is no such thing
     as an individual
But it is worth the effort
To finally find yourself in others
It is not easy to accept that none of us really exists
Except when we exist for each other
But why live only for yourself when you might as
     well be dead?

It is not impossible to gain a whole world
In the breathless chase for everything
But what can you do with a world
If you lost your soul in getting it

It is not easy to believe that you cannot buy your
     life or own your life
That the more of it you consume, the more alive
     you will feel

Because this is the ocean we swim in,
the shimmering liquid mirage our evolutionary
        pilgrimage has adapted us to
And coming up for air might drown us

It is not easy to realise *ubuntu*
That 'I am because you are', that unless you are,
        I am not
But unless we do and until we can
Maybe none of us will really ever be

It is not easy to follow a call instead of a career
(If they do not overlap)
But it is the pearl of great price to find your heart
In tune with the universe

It is not easy to lose your life
Without becoming dead
It is not easy to lose your life
But it is the only way to find it.

Martin Wroe

Purifier

I see who travels with me...

I want to change the fruits of my labours.

When someone says 'Apple', I don't want sleek plastic and chrome, but England's Coxes, heavy hung in dappled orchards.

When someone says 'Orange', I don't want to know about free minutes and the latest upgrades. I want to think citrus thoughts; the appeal of slowly peeling skin.

And when someone says 'Blackberry', I don't want my head to rush with virtual thoughts of emails and deadlines and documents and settings and schedules and coverage and battery life.

I want my tongue, instead, to rush with sweet sensation, a bowl of fruits shared with friends. A rug. Open space and blue sky.

Lech Walesa (leader of Poland's anti-communist movement in the 1980s) on coming to the West observed: 'You have riches and freedom here, but I feel no sense of faith or direction. You have so many computers, why don't you use them in the search for love?'

These devices were sold to connect me. But all I had to do was pick some fruit, and share it.

Kester Brewin

Late have I loved you,
beauty so old and so new:
late have I loved you.

And see, you were
within
and I was in the external world
and sought you there,

and in my unlovely state I plunged
into those lovely created things which you made.

You were with me,
and I was not with you.

The lovely things kept me
far from you,
though if they did not have their existence in you,
they had no existence at all.

You called
and cried aloud
and shattered my deafness.

You were radiant and resplendent,
you put to flight my blindness.

You were fragrant,
and I drew in my breath
and now pant after you.

I tasted you,
and I feel but hunger and thirst for you.

You touched me,
and I am on fire to attain
the peace
which is yours.

St Augustine of Hippo (354-430)

Background notes

Pages 12,13: Inspired by the famous and comforting words of Psalm 23, which describe God's provision and preservation of those who acknowledge him even in the bleakest times.

Page 15: Matthew's Gospel begins with the news that Jesus is to be 'God with us' (see 1:18–25) and finishes with Jesus assuring his followers as he sends them out to communicate his message: 'I am with you always, to the very end of the age' (28:20, TNIV). Many people say they have sensed his presence with them in lots of different ways, particularly to comfort them in times of loss.

Page 19: Sometimes sacrifice is necessary to allow a situation or person to reach their full potential. Jesus embodied this by dying to give others life: '… unless a grain of wheat falls to the ground and dies, it remains only a single seed. But if it dies, it produces many seeds' (John 12:24, TNIV).

Pages 20,21: Many people regret the way they parted from someone who is now dead. The details of the next life are beyond our grasp, although the apostle Paul turns the implications of death on their head. The Christian experience of death is seen as the loss of what is weak and imperfect in human life in favour of what is imperishable and immortal (see 1 Corinthians 15:35–57). Paul also writes about the part God can play in reconciliation and forgiveness in this life in 2 Corinthians 5:17–19.

Pages 24,25: This reflection is a small quarrel with the misuse of Paul's words, 'Where, O death, is your victory? Where, O death, is your sting?' (1 Corinthians 15:55, TNIV). His intention is to describe the joyful hope that the follower of Christ has in resurrection, not to separate the reader from the rawness of loss.

Pages 28,29: Based on the story of two disciples on the road to Emmaus in Luke 24:13–35. Although closely related to the resurrection narrative of the Gospels, on another level it reminds us of the hope available, for those who want it, of a personal God who walks with us in our grief.

Pages 32,33: Traditionally, King Solomon is regarded as the author of Proverbs, Song of Songs and Ecclesiastes in the Bible. This reflection was also inspired by the apostle Paul's inspiring and famous words, now a common feature of many wedding ceremonies, but originally written to a troubled community in Corinth: 'Love does not delight in evil but rejoices with the truth. It always protects, always trusts, always hopes, always perseveres. Love never fails' (1 Corinthians 13:6–8, TNIV). This is not the woolly love of the starry-eyed romantic, but the practical self-giving love of a true friend, which for Paul was personified in the selfless life and death of Jesus Christ.

Pages 36,37: This is a reflection on the power of generous, selfless giving, called 'grace' in the New Testament Scriptures. In a world where relationships were often framed by calculated legal rules and transactions, Paul explained that '... by grace you have been saved through faith, and this is not your own doing; it is the gift of God' (Ephesians 2:8, NRSV).

Page 39: The biblical book of Ecclesiastes tells us that weeping, laughing, birth and death are all inevitable seasons in life (see 3:1–8). The apostle Paul suggests that the whole of creation is, in a sense, in a state of painful transition like childbirth, but that this anticipates a liberation, which, while bringing fullness of life for those who persevered in their commitment to Christ, will impact all creation (see Romans 8:18–23).

Pages 44,45: The dislocation and brokenness of urban life is often exposed by a particular shocking and tragic event. In the biblical book Lamentations the spiritual bankruptcy of the people of God's beloved city, Jerusalem, ultimately brings disaster through God's judgement, and the city herself is given a voice to express the tragedy: 'Look, O LORD, and see how worthless I have become. Is it nothing to you, all you who pass by?' (1:11,12, NRSV).

Pages 48,49: The account of creation in the book of Genesis presents us with a humankind that, although formed from the dirt of the earth, is in intimate relationship with the divine Creator. Human wilfulness then destroys this closeness, and the story of God's subsequent dealings with people focuses on his efforts to restore the relationship (see John 3:16–18).

Pages 52,53: Going right back to the book of Genesis, the image of uprooted nomads, living as 'strangers' and 'exiles', occurs again and again in the Judeo-Christian Scriptures. Sometimes this uprooting is voluntary, sometimes forced (see Psalm 137).

Page 55: This reflection is inspired by the parable of the lost son in Luke 15:11–32, which demonstrates the patience and forgiveness of God, who is a Father who looks for us and wants to take us home.

Pages 60,61: The parable of the lost coin (see Luke 15:8–10) describes the value of people to God in terms of extravagant concern about a seemingly insubstantial loss.

Pages 64,65: The opening statement comes from Jesus' teaching in Luke 9:23–25 concerning the necessary sacrifices involved in following him in order to experience the full blessings of being his disciple. His teaching is always practical for life, eg 'If you accumulate loads of stuff on earth,' he said, 'someone will only break in and steal it, or it'll break or rust. There are more rewarding and important things to focus on in life' (see Matthew 6:19–21).

Page 67: Those entering mid-life can often feel the opportunity to 'be somebody' has left them. Perhaps this is a time to reflect on what really matters. Jesus identifies himself as the focus of the devoted life, issuing the challenge: 'What good is it for you to gain the whole world, and yet lose or forfeit your very self?' (see Luke 9:23–25, TNIV).

Pages 68,69: Archbishop Desmond Tutu describes a person practising the African concept *ubuntu* as one who '… is open and available to others, affirming of others, does not feel threatened that others are able and good, for he or she has a proper self-assurance that comes from knowing that he or she belongs to a greater whole and is diminished when others are humiliated or diminished …' This idea can be taken even further by practising the Christian teaching of loving both your neighbour and your enemy (see Matthew 5:43–45; 22:39).

Page 71: The book of Galatians (chapter 5) in the Bible describes a life full of God as being characterised by fruitfulness; 'love, joy, peace, patience and kindness' will grow and be seen and enjoyed by others. With so many technologies alluding to nature in their logos and names, it would be nice if we had these biblical fruits in mind as we emailed and texted our way through each day.

Acknowledgements

The Editor would like to thank the following for their help with the development of *Wise Traveller*: John Drane, Ray Simpson, Jonny Baker, Lizzie Green, Venetia Horton and, especially, Matt Campbell, whose contribution to the series is incalculable!

Original writing

Pages 12,13,68,69 © Martin Wroe. Martin makes a living as a journalist, makes a loss writing prayers and is a trustee of the Greenbelt arts festival.

Pages 15,19,32,33,39 © Sue Wallace. Sue is music and arts co-ordinator for Visions in York. www.visions-york.org

Pages 20,21,28,29,55,67 © Steve Hollinghurst. Steve lives in Manchester and works in Sheffield as a researcher. onearthasinheaven.blogspot.com

Pages 24,25,36,37,44,45,60,61 © John Davies. John is an Evertonian with a high tolerance for suffering. He is also a vicar. www.johndavies.org

Pages 48,49,64,65,71 © Kester Brewin. Kester is a writer and part-time Maths teacher at a London high school. He is the author of *The Complex Christ* and a founder member of Vaux – 'a community of artists and city-lovers exploring a spirituality of the city'. http://kester.typepad.com/signs/

Pages 52,53 Matt Campbell. Matt is the author of the underrated children's classic, *God made snot!*

Scripture Union takes no responsibility for the content of websites and blogs listed here that it does not directly operate. For further information about *Wise Traveller*: www.wisetraveller.org.uk

Quotations

Research by Andrew Clark, Mark Laynesmith, Carsten Lorenz and Ellen Wakeham.

Page 5 David Adam, 'Listen', *Wisdom is calling*, edited by Geoffrey Duncan (Canterbury Press, 1999).

Pages 7,8 'St Patrick's Breastplate', translated by CF Alexander (1906).

Page 11 Simone Weil, 'The Love of God and Affliction', *Waiting on God* (Routledge and Kegan Paul, 1951).

Pages 16,17,41,47 RS Thomas, 'The Presence', 'The Kingdom', 'Via Negativa', *Collected Poems, 1945–1990* (JM Dent, a division of The Orion Publishing Group, 2000).

Page 23 St Gregory of Nazianzus, from *Nicene and Post-Nicene Fathers*, 2nd Series, edited by P Schaff and H Wace (Wm B Eerdmans, 1955). Reprinted with permission of the publisher.

Page 27 © Pat Bennett, 'In this darkness' from *I will not sing alone: Songs for the seasons of love* (Wild Goose Resource Group, 2004).

Page 31 St John of Damascus, from the rite of burial as used in the Orthodox Church (translation from the Greek Orthodox Archdiocese of America).

Page 35 Martin Luther King, Jr, 'On being a good neighbour', quoted in *Strength to Love* (Fount, 1987).

Page 40 Henri Nouwen, taken from *Reaching Out* by Henri Nouwen. Copyright © 1998. Used by permission of Zondervan.

Pages 43,74,75,77 Scripture quotations taken from the HOLY BIBLE, TODAY'S NEW INTERNATIONAL VERSION. Copyright